MEXICAN COOKING

DISCOVER SIMPLE MEXICAN COOKING WITH EASY MEXICAN RECIPES

By
BookSumo Press
Copyright © by Saxonberg Associates

Published by
BookSumo Press, a DBA of Saxonberg Associates
http://www.booksumo.com/

ABOUT THE AUTHOR.

BookSumo Press is a publisher of unique, easy, and healthy cookbooks.

Our cookbooks span all topics and all subjects. If you want a deep dive into the possibilities of cooking with any type of ingredient. Then BookSumo Press is your go to place for robust yet simple and delicious cookbooks and recipes. Whether you are looking for great tasting pressure cooker recipes or authentic ethic and cultural food. BookSumo Press has a delicious and easy cookbook for you.

With simple ingredients, and even simpler step-by-step instructions BookSumo cookbooks get everyone in the kitchen chefing delicious meals.

BookSumo is an independent publisher of books operating in the beautiful Garden State (NJ) and our team of chefs and kitchen experts are here to teach, eat, and be merry!

INTRODUCTION

Welcome to *The Effortless Chef Series*! Thank you for taking the time to purchase this cookbook.

Come take a journey into the delights of easy cooking. The point of this cookbook and all BookSumo Press cookbooks is to exemplify the effortless nature of cooking simply.

In this book we focus on Mexican. You will find that even though the recipes are simple, the taste of the dishes are quite amazing.

So will you take an adventure in simple cooking? If the answer is yes please consult the table of contents to find the dishes you are most interested in.

Once you are ready, jump right in and start cooking.

— BookSumo Press

TABLE OF CONTENTS

ANY ISSUES? CONTACT US

If you find that something important to you is missing from this book please contact us at info@booksumo.com.

We will take your concerns into consideration when the 2nd edition of this book is published. And we will keep you updated!

— BookSumo Press

LEGAL NOTES

COMMON ABBREVIATIONS

cup(s)	C.
tablespoon	tbsp
teaspoon	tsp
ounce	oz.
pound	lb

*All units used are standard American measurements

CHAPTER 1: EASY MEXICAN RECIPES

MEXICO CITY QUESADILLAS

Ingredients

- 1/2 lb. ground beef
- 1/2 red onion, diced
- 1 clove garlic, minced
- 1 pinch salt
- 1 C. shredded Cheddar cheese, divided
- 1/4 C. shredded mozzarella cheese
- 1 tbsp milk
- 1 tbsp butter, divided
- 2 (12 inch) flour tortillas
- 2 tbsp Thousand Island dressing, divided
- 1 romaine lettuce heart, sliced
- 1 tomato, sliced
- 1/2 red onion, sliced

Directions

- Heat a large skillet and cook the beef, diced onion and garlic for about 5-8 minutes.

- Stir in the salt and transfer the beef mixture into a pan on low heat.
- Add 3/4 C. of the Cheddar cheese, mozzarella cheese and milk and Cook, stirring for about 3-5 minutes.
- In a large skillet, melt half of the butter on medium heat and cook 1 tortilla for about 3 minutes.
- Flip the tortilla and spread 1 tbsp dressing over the tortilla evenly.
- Place half of the beef mixture over the tortilla and fold in half.
- Cook for about 1-2 minutes per side.
- Transfer into a serving plate.
- Repeat with second tortilla.
- Sprinkle the remaining 1/4 C. of the Cheddar cheese over the tortillas.
- Keep aside to cool for about 5 minutes.
- Cut into the wedges and serve with the lettuce, tomato and sliced onion.

Amount per serving (4 total)

Timing Information:

Preparation	20 m
Cooking	13 m
Total Time	38 m

Nutritional Information:

Calories	521 kcal
Fat	30 g
Carbohydrates	38.4g
Protein	24.4 g
Cholesterol	79 mg
Sodium	777 mg

* Percent Daily Values are based on a 2,000 calorie diet.

Maria's Quesadillas

Ingredients

- 1 (15 oz.) can black beans, drained
- 1 tbsp vegetable oil
- 1/2 onion, chopped
- 1 red bell pepper, chopped
- 1 tsp chili powder
- 1 pinch cayenne pepper
- 1 pinch dried oregano
- 1 pinch dried basil
- 1 mango - peeled, seeded and diced
- 1 (6 oz.) package seasoned chicken-style vegetarian strips
- 6 (10 inch) flour tortillas
- 1 (8 oz.) package shredded Cheddar cheese
- 1 C. arugula leaves
- 1 (4 oz.) jar jalapeno pepper rings (optional)
- 1 (8 oz.) jar salsa

Directions

- In a pan, place the beans on medium heat and cook for about 5 minutes.
- With a potato masher, mash the beans partially.

- Reduce the heat to low and keep warm until ready to serve.
- In a skillet, heat the oil on medium heat and sauté the onion, red bell pepper, chili powder, cayenne pepper, oregano and basil till tender.
- Stir in the mango and vegetarian chicken strips and cook for about 2 minutes.
- Heat another skillet on medium heat and cook the tortillas for about 2 minutes per side.
- Place the black beans over warm tortillas, followed by the mango mixture, Cheddar cheese, arugula and jalapeño.
- Fold the tortillas over the filling and top with the salsa to serve.

Amount per serving (6 total)

Timing Information:

Preparation	10 m
Cooking	20 m
Total Time	30 m

Nutritional Information:

Calories	503 kcal
Fat	24.2 g
Carbohydrates	49.2g
Protein	23.2 g
Cholesterol	39 mg
Sodium	1421 mg

* Percent Daily Values are based on a 2,000 calorie diet.

Mushroom Chicken and Bacon Quesadillas

Ingredients

- 1 lb. thinly sliced chicken breast meat
- 1/2 tsp salt
- 1/2 tsp ground black pepper
- 2 tbsp olive oil
- 14 slices cooked turkey bacon, chopped
- 1 (8 oz.) package sliced fresh mushrooms
- 1 C. Alfredo sauce
- 1 tsp butter
- 5 large flour tortillas
- 2 C. shredded mozzarella cheese

Directions

- Sprinkle the chicken with the salt and black pepper.
- In a large skillet, heat the olive oil on medium heat and cook the chicken for about 8-10 minutes.
- Remove the chicken from the skillet and keep aside.
- Discard any excess grease from the pan.
- In the same skillet, add the bacon and mushrooms on medium heat and cook for about 5 minutes.

- Reduce the heat to low.
- Cut the chicken into bite-size strips.
- Add the Alfredo sauce and chicken strips into the skillet and simmer for a few minutes.
- In another skillet, melt the butter and place a tortilla in the melted butter.
- Place about 1/5 of the chicken Alfredo mixture onto 1 half of warm tortilla.
- Sprinkle about 1/5 of the mozzarella cheese over the chicken alfredo mixture.
- Fold the tortilla in half and cook for about 3-5 minutes.
- Carefully flip the quesadilla and cook for about 3-5 minutes.
- Repeat with the remaining tortillas and filling.
- Slice the quesadillas into thirds to serve.

Amount per serving (5 total)

Timing Information:

Preparation	20 m
Cooking	30 m
Total Time	50 m

Nutritional Information:

Calories	880 kcal
Fat	46.2 g
Carbohydrates	65.6g
Protein	49.6 g
Cholesterol	121 mg
Sodium	2178 mg

* Percent Daily Values are based on a 2,000 calorie diet.

Southern Quesadillas

Ingredients

- 1 tbsp butter
- 1 tbsp olive oil
- 1/2 red bell pepper, diced
- 4 green onions, sliced thin
- 1 tbsp fajita seasoning
- 1/2 tsp cayenne pepper
- 12 oz. cooked and peeled whole crawfish tails
- 6 (10 inch) flour tortillas
- 8 oz. crumbled queso fresco cheese
- 1 tbsp butter
- 1 tbsp olive oil

Directions

- In a skillet, melt 1 tbsp of the butter and 1 tbsp of the olive oil in a skillet on medium heat and sauté the bell pepper, green onions, fajita seasoning and cayenne pepper for about 4 minutes.
- Add the crawfish tails and cook a few more minutes and keep aside.
- Place the tortillas onto a smooth surface and place about half of the queso fresco onto one side of each tortilla.

- Place the crawfish mixture on top of the cheese evenly and sprinkle with the remaining cheese.
- Fold the tortillas over the filling, pressing down lightly.
- In a large skillet, melt 1 tsp of the butter and 1 tsp of the olive oil on medium heat and cook two of the quesadillas for about 3 minutes per side.
- Repeat with the remaining butter, olive oil and quesadillas.
- Cut into wedges to serve.

Amount per serving (6 total)

Timing Information:

Preparation	20 m
Cooking	30 m
Total Time	50 m

Nutritional Information:

Calories	396 kcal
Fat	17.5 g
Carbohydrates	40.1g
Protein	18.9 g
Cholesterol	82 mg
Sodium	628 mg

* Percent Daily Values are based on a 2,000 calorie diet.

Mexican Mountain Quesadillas

Ingredients

- 1/2 C. salsa, divided
- 4 (10 inch) flour tortillas
- 1/4 C. chopped sweet onion
- 1/4 C. chopped green bell pepper
- 1/4 C. chopped red bell pepper
- 1/4 C. chopped tomato
- 2 tbsp chopped fresh cilantro
- 2 tbsp chopped fresh chives
- 1/4 C. sliced black olives
- 1 C. cooked and peeled shrimp
- 1/2 C. shredded Cheddar cheese
- 1/4 C. sour cream

Directions

- Set your outdoor grill for low heat and lightly, grease the grill grate.
- Spread 1 tbsp of salsa on half of each tortilla, followed by the onion, green bell pepper, red bell pepper, tomato, cilantro, chives, olives and shrimp evenly.

- Sprinkle with the cheese and fold the tortillas in half to cover the filling.
- Cook the tortillas on the grill for about 2 minutes per side.
- Serve with remaining salsa and sour cream.

Amount per serving (4 total)

Timing Information:

Preparation	20 m
Cooking	10 m
Total Time	30 m

Nutritional Information:

Calories	374 kcal
Fat	14.8 g
Carbohydrates	41.8g
Protein	18.8 g
Cholesterol	86 mg
Sodium	906 mg

* Percent Daily Values are based on a 2,000 calorie diet.

Tex-Mex Quesadillas

Ingredients

- 1 tbsp vegetable oil
- 1 onion, finely diced
- 2 cloves garlic, minced
- 1 (15 oz.) can black beans, rinsed and drained
- 1 green bell pepper, chopped
- 2 tomatoes, chopped
- 1/2 (10 oz.) package frozen corn
- 12 (12 inch) flour tortillas
- 1 C. shredded Cheddar cheese
- 1/4 C. vegetable oil

Directions

- In a large skillet, heat the oil on medium heat and sauté the onion and garlic till tender.
- Add the beans, bell pepper, tomatoes and corn and cook till heated completely.
- Spread the bean and vegetable mixture over 6 tortillas evenly.
- Sprinkle with the Cheddar cheese evenly and top with the remaining tortillas to form quesadillas.

- In a large skillet, heat 1/4 C. of the oil on medium-high heat and cook the quesadillas till golden browned from both sides, turning once.

Amount per serving (12 total)

Timing Information:

Preparation	15 m
Cooking	30 m
Total Time	45 m

Nutritional Information:

Calories	504 kcal
Fat	18.3 g
Carbohydrates	69.7g
Protein	14.7 g
Cholesterol	10 mg
Sodium	913 mg

* Percent Daily Values are based on a 2,000 calorie diet.

CHIPOTLE SALSA

Ingredients

- 2 ears corn on the cob, husks and silk removed
- 2 tomatoes, chopped
- 2 avocados - peeled, pitted, and diced
- 1/2 bunch cilantro, stems cut off and leaves chopped
- 1 white onion, chopped
- 3 tablespoons chopped garlic
- 2 tablespoons olive oil
- 2 tablespoons red wine vinegar
- kosher salt to taste

Directions

- Get an outdoor grill hot and coat the grate with oil.
- Place your corn on the grate once the grill is hot and cook the corn for 4 mins each side. Turn the ears constantly to avoid any burning. After you have completely grilled the corn slice off the kernel into a bowl. Let the kernel sit until they have lost their heat.
- Once the corn has cooled off combine in the: red vinegar, tomatoes, olive oil, avocados, garlic, white onion, and cilantro. Toss everything then combine in the kosher salt and toss everything again.

- Enjoy.

Amount per serving 6

Timing Information:

Preparation	30 m
Cooking	15 m
Total Time	55 m

Nutritional Information:

Calories	198 kcal
Fat	14.8 g
Carbohydrates	17g
Protein	3.3 g
Cholesterol	0 mg
Sodium	82 mg

* Percent Daily Values are based on a 2,000 calorie diet.

Lunch Box Salad

Ingredients

Dressing:

- 1/2 cup mayonnaise
- 3 small green onions, thinly sliced
- 2 tablespoons white wine vinegar
- 2 tablespoons minced pickled jalapeno peppers
- 2 tablespoons minced fresh parsley
- 1 tablespoon light olive oil
- salt and ground black pepper to taste

Vegetables:

- 2 (11 ounce) cans shoepeg corn, rinsed and drained
- 1 cup halved grape tomatoes

Directions

- Get a bowl, combine: olive oil, mayo, parsley, green onion, jalapeno, and vinegar. Work the mix completely then combine in some pepper and salt.
- Now stir in your tomatoes and corn into the mayo mix. Place a covering of plastic on the bowl and put everything in the fridge for 4 hours.
- Enjoy.

Amount per serving 8

Timing Information:

Preparation	15 m
Total Time	4 h 15 m

Nutritional Information:

Calories	201 kcal
Fat	13.3 g
Carbohydrates	18g
Protein	2.4 g
Cholesterol	5 mg
Sodium	340 mg

* Percent Daily Values are based on a 2,000 calorie diet.

How to Grill Corn

Ingredients

- 5 cloves garlic, minced, or more to taste
- 1/2 cup butter
- 1 tablespoon white sugar
- 1 teaspoon salt
- 1 teaspoon ground cumin
- 1 teaspoon ground black pepper
- 1/2 lime, juiced
- 2 tablespoons hot pepper sauce (such as Tapatio(R))
- 6 ears fresh corn

Directions

- Get your grill hot outside and coat the grate with oil.
- Add your butter and garlic to a little pot and let the mix melt for 7 mins but make sure the mix does not begin to bubble.
- Get a bowl and combine: cumin, sugar, black pepper, and salt. Stir the spice mix evenly then combine it with the butter mix then add in the lime juice and combine everything again then add in the hot sauce and stir again. Coat your corn with the sauce and reserve the rest.

- Grill the coated corn pieces for about 12 mins flipping the ear and grilling each part evenly. Coat the ears as they cook with the reserved mixture.
- Enjoy.

Amount per serving 6

Timing Information:

Preparation	15 m
Cooking	15 m
Total Time	30 m

Nutritional Information:

Calories	229 kcal
Fat	16.5 g
Carbohydrates	21.1g
Protein	3.4 g
Cholesterol	41 mg
Sodium	635 mg

* Percent Daily Values are based on a 2,000 calorie diet.

AUTHENTIC MEXICAN CORN

Ingredients

- 4 slices turkey bacon
- 4 ears fresh sweet corn, kernels cut from the cob
- 1 teaspoon ground cumin
- 1/4 teaspoon sea salt
- 1/4 teaspoon ground cayenne pepper
- 1 small onion, chopped
- 1/2 small red bell pepper, chopped
- 2 cloves garlic, chopped
- 1/4 cup chicken broth
- 1/4 cup crumbled cotija cheese
- 1/4 cup chopped fresh cilantro

Directions

- Fry your turkey bacon in a frying pan for about 8 to 12 mins until they are fully cooked then remove any excess oils. Place the bacon on some plates covered with paper towel then dice the bacon into pieces.
- Add your pieces of corn into a frying pan and top them with the cayenne, cumin, and sea salt. Stir fry the kernels with a high level of heat then add in the garlic, onion, and bell pepper. Stir everything then add in the chicken and

scrape the pan to remove the browned bits. Continue to stir fry everything for about 18 to 20 mins until the pieces of corn are dark and everything is soft.

- Shut the heat and combine in the cilantro, cotija, and bacon and toss the mix.
- Enjoy.

Amount per serving 4

Timing Information:

Preparation	30 m
Cooking	40 m
Total Time	1 h 10 m

Nutritional Information:

Calories	179 kcal
Fat	7.5 g
Carbohydrates	21.3g
Protein	8.6 g
Cholesterol	19 mg
Sodium	429 mg

* Percent Daily Values are based on a 2,000 calorie diet.

CREAMY CORN 101

Ingredients

- 1 1/2 (8 ounce) packages cream cheese
- 1/2 cup milk
- 1/4 cup butter
- 1 teaspoon garlic salt
- 4 (12 ounce) cans whole kernel corn, drained
- 3 (4 ounce) cans chopped green chilies
- 1 (4 ounce) can chopped jalapeno peppers

Directions

- Set your oven to 350 degrees before doing anything else.
- Get a pot and combine: garlic salt, cream cheese, butter, and milk. Stir and heat the mix for 7 mins then combine in the jalapenos, corn, and green chilies. Stir the mix again then pour everything into a casserole dish.
- Let everything cook for 32 mins in the oven.
- Enjoy.

Amount per serving 10

Timing Information:

Preparation	10 m
Cooking	35 m
Total Time	45 m

Nutritional Information:

Calories	285 kcal
Fat	18 g
Carbohydrates	29.4g
Protein	7 g
Cholesterol	50 mg
Sodium	1306 mg

* Percent Daily Values are based on a 2,000 calorie diet.

New Mexican Corn Cake

Ingredients

- 1/2 cup butter, softened
- 1/3 cup masa harina
- 1/4 cup water
- 1 1/2 cups frozen whole-kernel corn, thawed
- 1/4 cup cornmeal
- 1/3 cup white sugar
- 2 tablespoons heavy whipping cream
- 1/4 teaspoon salt
- 1/2 teaspoon baking powder

Directions

- Set your oven to 350 degrees before doing anything else.
- Get a bowl, and whisk your butter in it until the butter is soft and creamy. Combine in the water, and corn flour, and continue to whisk everything.
- Add your corn to a blender and pulse the corn until it is chopped evenly and chunky. Then combine it with the butter mix.
- Get a 2nd bowl, combine: baking powder, cornmeal, salt, sugar, and cream. Combine this with your processed corn and stir then enter everything into an 8 x 8 dish.

- Place a covering of foil on the dish and put the smaller dish into a casserole dish. Fill about 75% of the casserole dish with some water and cook everything in the oven for 1 hr.
- Enjoy.

Amount per serving 6

Timing Information:

Preparation	15 m
Cooking	1 h
Total Time	1 h 15 m

Nutritional Information:

Calories	273 kcal
Fat	18.1 g
Carbohydrates	27.9g
Protein	2.6 g
Cholesterol	47 mg
Sodium	257 mg

* Percent Daily Values are based on a 2,000 calorie diet.

LINDA MAE'S CHOWDER

Ingredients

- 2 tablespoons margarine
- 1 cup chopped celery
- 1 cup chopped onion
- 2 (14.5 ounce) cans chicken broth
- 3 cups peeled and cubed potatoes
- 1 (15 ounce) can whole kernel corn
- 1 (4 ounce) can diced green chills
- 1 (2.5 ounce) package country style gravy mix
- 2 cups milk
- 1 cup shredded Mexican-style processed cheese food

Directions

- Get your margarine hot in a pot then combine in the onion and celery. Let the mix cook for 7 mins then combine in the chicken broth and get everything boiling. Once the mix is boiling combine in the potatoes and let the mix cook for 23 mins. Stir the mix at least 3 to 4 times evenly.
- Now add in the chilies and corn and get everything boiling again.

- Get a bowl and combine your milk and milk gravy mix then add the mix to the corn mix and also combine in the cheese and let everything cook until the cheese fully combined in.
- Enjoy.

Amount per serving 7

Timing Information:

Preparation	20 m
Cooking	35 m
Total Time	55 m

Nutritional Information:

Calories	289 kcal
Fat	11.8 g
Carbohydrates	37.8g
Protein	11.3 g
Cholesterol	23 mg
Sodium	1021 mg

* Percent Daily Values are based on a 2,000 calorie diet.

CANCUN STYLE CAVIAR

Ingredients

- 2 large tomatoes, finely chopped
- 5 green onions, chopped
- 3 tbsp olive oil
- 3 1/2 tbsp tarragon vinegar
- 1 (4 oz.) can chopped green chili peppers
- 1 (2.25 oz.) can chopped black olives
- 1 tsp garlic salt
- 1 tsp salt

Directions

- In a medium bowl, mix together all the ingredients.
- Refrigerate, covered for about 6 hours or overnight before serving.

Amount per serving (32 total)

Timing Information:

| Preparation | 10 m |
| Total Time | 6 h 10 m |

Nutritional Information:

Calories	17 kcal
Fat	1.5 g
Cholesterol	0.9g
Sodium	0.2 g
Carbohydrates	0 mg
Protein	188 mg

* Percent Daily Values are based on a 2,000 calorie diet.

PEPPERJACK PIZZA

Ingredients

- 1/2 (16 oz.) can spicy fat-free refried beans
- 1 C. salsa, divided
- 1 (12 inch) pre-baked Italian pizza crust
- 2 C. shredded hearts of romaine lettuce
- 3 medium green onions, thinly sliced
- 1/4 C. ranch dressing
- 1/4 C. crumbled tortilla chips
- 1 C. shredded pepper Jack cheese

Directions

- Set your oven to 450 degrees F before doing anything else and arrange a rack in the lowest portion of the oven.
- In a bowl, mix together the beans and 1/2 C. of the salsa.
- Arrange the crust on a cookie sheet and top with the bean mixture evenly.
- Cook in the oven for about 10 minutes.
- Remove from the oven and place the lettuce, green onions over the beans mixture.
- Top with the remaining salsa.

- Drizzle with the dressing evenly and top with the chips and cheese evenly.
- Cook in the oven for about 2 minutes more.
- Cut into 6 slices and serve.

Amount per serving (6 total)

Timing Information:

Preparation	20 m
Cooking	12 m
Total Time	32 m

Nutritional Information:

Calories	373 kcal
Fat	15.3 g
Carbohydrates	44g
Protein	17 g
Cholesterol	26 mg
Sodium	1027 mg

* Percent Daily Values are based on a 2,000 calorie diet.

Puerto Vallarta Eggplant

Ingredients

- 1 lb. ground beef
- 1/4 C. chopped onion
- 1 tbsp all-purpose flour
- 1 (8 oz.) can tomato sauce
- 1/4 C. chopped green bell pepper
- 1 tsp dried oregano
- 1 tsp chili powder
- 1 eggplant, cut into 1/2-inch slices
- salt and ground black pepper to taste
- 1 C. shredded Cheddar cheese

Directions

- Heat a large skillet on medium-high heat and cook the ground beef and onion for about 5-7 minutes.
- Drain the grease from the skillet.
- Sprinkle the flour over the beef mixture and toss to coat.
- Stir in the tomato sauce, green bell pepper, oregano and chili powder.
- Sprinkle the eggplant slices with the salt and pepper and place over the beef mixture.

- Simmer, covered for about 10-15 minutes.
- Serve with a topping of the Cheddar cheese.

Amount per serving (4 total)

Timing Information:

Preparation	10 m
Cooking	15 m
Total Time	25 m

Nutritional Information:

Calories	349 kcal
Fat	23.3 g
Carbohydrates	6.8g
Protein	27.4 g
Cholesterol	101 mg
Sodium	542 mg

* Percent Daily Values are based on a 2,000 calorie diet.

Mexican Veggie Puree

Ingredients

- 6 spears fresh asparagus, trimmed and cut into 1/2 inch pieces
- 1 C. bite-size cauliflower florets
- 2 stalks celery ribs, chopped
- 1/3 C. canned kidney beans, drained
- 1/3 C. chopped hazelnuts
- 2/3 tsp chopped fresh dill
- 1/4 tsp dried basil
- 1/2 tsp minced garlic
- 2 tbsp sunflower seed oil
- 1/3 tsp chili powder
- 1/4 tsp celery seed
- 1/2 tsp salt

Directions

- Steam the asparagus and cauliflower for about 10 minutes.
- Transfer the vegetables into a bowl and stir in the celery.

- In a blender, add the kidney beans, hazelnuts, dill, basil, garlic, oil, chili powder, celery seed and salt and pulse till smooth.
- Pour the sauce over the vegetables mixture and serve

Amount per serving (4 total)

Timing Information:

Preparation	25 m
Cooking	10 m
Total Time	35 m

Nutritional Information:

Calories	167 kcal
Fat	14.1 g
Carbohydrates	8.3g
Protein	4.1 g
Cholesterol	0 mg
Sodium	363 mg

* Percent Daily Values are based on a 2,000 calorie diet.

CLASSICAL MEXICAN CEVICHE

Ingredients

- 5 large lemons, juiced
- 1 lb. jumbo shrimp, peeled and deveined
- 1/4 C. chopped fresh cilantro
- tomato and clam juice cocktail
- 2 white onions, finely chopped
- 1 cucumber, peeled and finely chopped
- 1 large tomatoes, seeded and chopped
- 3 fresh jalapeno peppers, seeded and minced
- 1 bunch radishes, finely diced
- 2 cloves fresh garlic, minced
- tortilla chips

Directions

- In a bowl, add the shrimp and enough lemon juice to cover the shrimp completely.
- Refrigerate, covered for about 30 minutes.
- Remove the bowl of shrimp from the refrigerator.
- Add the tomatoes, onions, cucumber, radishes and garlic and toss to coat.
- Slowly, stir in the cilantro and jalapeño peppers.

- Stir in the tomato and clam juice and refrigerate, covered for about 1 hour.
- Serve chilled with the tortilla chips.

Amount per serving (8 total)

Timing Information:

Preparation	30 m
Cooking	30 m
Total Time	2 h

Nutritional Information:

Calories	387 kcal
Fat	12.4 g
Carbohydrates	57.6g
Protein	17.7 g
Cholesterol	86 mg
Sodium	733 mg

* Percent Daily Values are based on a 2,000 calorie diet.

HONEY & BEANS LATIN SALAD

Ingredients

- 1 (15 oz.) can black beans, rinsed and drained
- 1 (15 oz.) can garbanzo beans, drained
- 2 C. frozen corn kernels
- 1/2 onion, finely diced
- 1 tbsp chopped fresh cilantro
- 2 jalapeno peppers, seeded and minced (optional)
- 1 red bell pepper, diced
- 1/4 C. olive oil
- 3 tbsp fresh lime juice
- 1 tsp ground black pepper
- salt to taste
- 1/2 tsp honey

Directions

- In a large bowl, add all the ingredients and mix well.
- Refrigerate till the flavors blends completely.

Amount per serving (6 total)

Timing Information:

Preparation	20 m
Total Time	40 m

Nutritional Information:

Calories	10.6 g
Fat	34.8g
Cholesterol	8.2 g
Sodium	0 mg
Carbohydrates	358 mg
Protein	10.6 g

* Percent Daily Values are based on a 2,000 calorie diet.

Taco Tuesday's Lasagna

Ingredients

- 1 lb. lean ground beef
- 1 (1 oz.) package taco seasoning mix
- 1 (14 oz.) can peeled and diced tomatoes with juice
- 10 (6 inch) corn tortillas
- 1 C. prepared salsa
- 1/2 C. shredded Colby cheese

Directions

- Set your oven to 350 degrees F before doing anything else.
- Heat a large skillet on medium-high heat and cook the beef till browned completely.
- Stir in the taco seasoning and tomatoes.
- In the bottom of a 13x9-inch baking dish, arrange half of the tortillas evenly.
- Place the beef mixture over the tortillas evenly.
- Place the remaining tortillas over the beef mixture and top with the salsa, followed by the cheese.
- Cook in the oven for about 20-30 minutes.

Amount per serving (5 total)

Timing Information:

Preparation	25 m
Cooking	20 m
Total Time	45 m

Nutritional Information:

Calories	447 kcal
Fat	24 g
Carbohydrates	33.2g
Protein	23.2 g
Cholesterol	79 mg
Sodium	899 mg

* Percent Daily Values are based on a 2,000 calorie diet.

Coastal Mexican Enchiladas

Ingredients

- 5 tbsp olive oil
- 2 cloves minced garlic
- 1 tsp ground ginger
- 1/2 tsp hot sauce
- 16 large shrimp, peeled and deveined, without tails
- 4 (8 inch) flour tortillas
- 3/4 C. shredded Cheddar and Monterey cheese blend
- 2 C. fresh salsa

Directions

- In a large bowl, mix together 4 tbsp of the oil, garlic, ginger, hot sauce and shrimp.
- Add the shrimp and coat with the mixture generously.
- Refrigerate to marinate for about 2 hours.
- Set your oven to 350 degrees F before doing anything else and grease a 9-inch pie dish with the remaining 1 tbsp of the olive oil.
- Fill the flour tortillas with the marinated shrimp, cheese blend and salsa.

- Fold the tortillas into a roll and place in the prepared pie dish.
- Spread a thin layer of salsa on top of the tortillas.
- Cook in the oven for about 20 minutes.

Amount per serving (4 total)

Timing Information:

Preparation	2 h
Cooking	20 m
Total Time	2 h 20 m

Nutritional Information:

Calories	444 kcal
Fat	26.3 g
Carbohydrates	37.2g
Protein	16.6 g
Cholesterol	58 mg
Sodium	1234 mg

* Percent Daily Values are based on a 2,000 calorie diet.

GREAT ENCHILADAS

Ingredients

- 2 (16 oz.) jars prepared salsa
- 1 lb. ground beef
- 1 (15.5 oz.) jar prepared salsa con queso
- 20 (8 inch) flour tortillas
- 1 (8 oz.) package shredded Cheddar-Monterey Jack cheese blend

Directions

- Set your oven to 350 degrees F before doing anything else and grease a 13x9-inch baking dish.
- Place the salsa in the bottom of the prepared baking dish.
- Heat a large skillet on medium heat and cook the beef for about 10 minutes.
- Drain the excess grease from the skillet.
- Add the salsa con queso and stir to combine well.
- Place about 2 tbsp of the beef mixture in the center of each tortilla and roll the tortillas.
- Arrange the tortillas, seam side down on top of the salsa in the baking dish and sprinkle with the shredded cheese.
- Cook in the oven for about 15-20 minutes.

Amount per serving (10 total)

Timing Information:

Preparation	15 m
Cooking	30 m
Total Time	45 m

Nutritional Information:

Calories	595 kcal
Fat	25.8 g
Carbohydrates	68.3g
Protein	24.3 g
Cholesterol	54 mg
Sodium	1757 mg

* Percent Daily Values are based on a 2,000 calorie diet.

ENCHILADAS ITALIAN STYLE

Ingredients

- 2 lb. ground beef
- 1 large onion, chopped
- 2 (10.75 oz.) cans condensed cream of mushroom soup, undiluted
- 1 (1 lb.) loaf processed cheese food, cut into thin slices
- 2 (26 oz.) cans marinara sauce
- 2 (6.5 oz.) cans tomato sauce
- 3/4 C. water
- 20 (10 inch) flour tortillas

Directions

- Set your oven to 350 degrees F before doing anything else.
- Heat a large skillet on medium heat and cook the beef and onion till browned completely.
- Drain the excess grease from the skillet.
- Stir in the soup and cook till heated completely.
- In a bowl, mix together the marinara sauce, tomato sauce and water.
- Spread 1/3 of the mixture across the bottom of a 13x9-inch baking dish.

- Fill each tortilla with about 2 tbsp of the beef mixture and 2 slices cheese food.
- Tightly roll the tortillas and place the tortillas in the baking dish in 2 layers.
- Top with the remaining sauce mixture evenly followed by the remaining cheese food.
- Cover with the aluminum paper and cook in the oven for about 45 minutes.

Amount per serving (10 total)

Timing Information:

Preparation	25 m
Cooking	45 m
Total Time	1 h 10 m

Nutritional Information:

Calories	939 kcal
Fat	40.4 g
Carbohydrates	102.9g
Protein	39.3 g
Cholesterol	94 mg
Sodium	2694 mg

* Percent Daily Values are based on a 2,000 calorie diet.

CLASSICAL ENCHILADAS

Ingredients

- 2 lb. ground beef
- 1 onion, chopped
- 2 (4 oz.) cans chopped green chilies
- 1 (1 oz.) package taco seasoning
- 1 (16 oz.) container sour cream
- 2 (10.5 oz.) cans cream of chicken soup
- 12 flour tortillas
- 2 C. shredded Cheddar cheese
- 1 small tomato, chopped
- 1 1/2 C. shredded lettuce
- 1/4 C. black olives, sliced

Directions

- Set your oven to 350 degrees F before doing anything else.
- Heat a large skillet on medium heat and cook the beef, onion, 1 can green chilis, and taco seasoning for about 6-8 minutes.
- Drain the excess grease from the skillet.

- In a pan, mix together the sour cream, cream of chicken soup and 1 can of the green chilis on medium-low heat and simmer for about 10 minutes.
- Place about half of the warm sour cream mixture in the bottom of a 13x9-inch baking dish.
- Place the ground beef mixture in the center of each tortilla evenly.
- Roll tortillas and place on top of sour cream mixture in the baking dish.
- Place the remaining sour cream mixture over the tortillas and top with the Cheddar cheese.
- Cook in the oven for about 35 minutes.
- Serve the enchiladas with a topping of the lettuce, tomatoes and olives.

Amount per serving (12 total)

Timing Information:

Preparation	20 m
Cooking	55 m
Total Time	1 h 15 m

Nutritional Information:

Calories	588 kcal
Fat	32.1 g
Carbohydrates	47.4g
Protein	26.3 g
Cholesterol	88 mg
Sodium	1383 mg

* Percent Daily Values are based on a 2,000 calorie diet.

POTATOES CHEESE ENCHILADAS

Ingredients

- 3 tbsp vegetable oil
- 6 potatoes, peeled and shredded
- 1 (8 oz.) package processed cheese, melted
- 2 (10 oz.) cans diced tomatoes with green chili peppers, drained
- 1 (8 oz.) can sweet peas, drained
- 1 (8.75 oz.) can whole kernel corn, drained
- 12 (8 inch) flour tortillas

Directions

- In a large heavy skillet, heat oil on medium heat and cook the shredded potatoes till golden brown from both sides.
- In a small bowl mix together the melted processed cheese, diced tomatoes and chilis.
- Stir in half of the peas and half of the corn and mash them into the hash browns.
- Add the remaining peas and corn and mash till well combined.
- Stir in about 1 C. of the cheese and tomato mixture and mix well and cook for about 10 minutes.

- Place the potato mixture into the tortillas and roll like a burrito and smother with the cheese/tomato mixture.

Amount per serving (12 total)

Timing Information:

Preparation	20 m
Cooking	20 m
Total Time	40 m

Nutritional Information:

Calories	358 kcal
Fat	11.9 g
Carbohydrates	53g
Protein	10.8 g
Cholesterol	15 mg
Sodium	728 mg

* Percent Daily Values are based on a 2,000 calorie diet.

Italian Mackerel Enchiladas

Ingredients

- 1 lb. king mackerel fillets - cleaned, washed and cubed
- 1/2 C. Italian-style salad dressing
- 1/4 C. all-purpose flour
- 2 tbsp olive oil
- 1 onion, diced
- 1 green bell pepper, diced
- 1 (16 oz.) jar salsa
- 8 (8 inch) flour tortillas
- 8 oz. shredded Cheddar cheese

Directions

- In a bowl, mix together the fish cubes and Italian dressing and refrigerate to marinate for at least 30 minutes.
- Set your oven to 350 degrees F before doing anything else and grease a 13x9-inch baking dish.

- Dredge fish cubes in flour and keep aside.
- In a non-stick frying pan, heat olive oil on medium-high heat and cook the onions and green pepper till soft, stirring occasionally.
- Stir in the fish cubes and cook for about 5 minutes.
- Stir in half of the salsa and remove from the heat.
- Place the mixture into tortillas and roll them.
- In the prepared baking dish, place the tortillas, seam down.
- Place the remaining salsa over the enchiladas and sprinkle with the shredded cheese.
- Cook in the oven for about 15 minutes.

Amount per serving (8 total)

Timing Information:

Preparation	30 m
Cooking	30 m
Total Time	1 h

Nutritional Information:

Calories	445 kcal
Fat	21.7 g
Carbohydrates	37.9g
Protein	24.5 g
Cholesterol	60 mg
Sodium	1115 mg

* Percent Daily Values are based on a 2,000 calorie diet.

MAKE-AHEAD ENCHILADAS

Ingredients

- 1 lb. cooked ham, chopped
- 3/4 C. sliced green onions
- 3/4 C. chopped green bell peppers
- 3 C. shredded Cheddar cheese, divided
- 10 (7 inch) flour tortillas
- 5 eggs, beaten
- 2 C. half-and-half cream
- 1/2 C. milk
- 1 tbsp all-purpose flour
- 1/4 tsp garlic powder
- 1 dash hot pepper sauce

Directions

- Grease a 13x9-inch baking dish.
- In a food processor, add ham and pulse till finely ground.
- In a bowl, mix together the ham, green onions and green peppers.
- Place about 1/3 C. of the ham mixture and 3 tbsp of the shredded cheese onto each tortilla, then roll up.

- Carefully place the tortillas, seam side down, in the prepared baking dish.
- In a medium bowl, mix together the eggs, cream, milk, flour, garlic powder and hot pepper sauce.
- Place the egg mixture over the tortillas.
- Cover and refrigerate for about overnight.
- Set your oven to 350 degrees F.
- Cook in the oven for about 50-60 minutes.
- Sprinkle the casserole with remaining 1 C. of the shredded cheese and cook for about 3 minutes more.

Amount per serving (10 total)

Timing Information:

Preparation	30 m
Cooking	1 h
Total Time	9 h 30 m

Nutritional Information:

Calories	511 kcal
Fat	31.2 g
Carbohydrates	30.8g
Protein	26.2 g
Cholesterol	173 mg
Sodium	1104 mg

* Percent Daily Values are based on a 2,000 calorie diet.

AUTHENTIC TEXAS-MEXICAN ENCHILADAS

Ingredients

- 2 (11.25 oz.) cans chili without beans
- 1 C. enchilada sauce
- 1/2 C. vegetable oil
- 1 tbsp chili powder
- 15 corn tortillas
- 1 lb. shredded Cheddar cheese
- 1 onion, chopped

Directions

- Set your oven to 350 degrees F before doing anything else.
- In a small pan, mix the chili and enchilada sauce on medium-low heat and heat, stirring occasionally.
- In a small skillet, heat the vegetable oil and chili powder on medium heat and cook the tortillas, one at a time till they start to puff.
- Transfer the tortillas on a plate and immediately sprinkle with 1/4 C. of the Cheddar cheese and 1 tbsp of the chopped onion in the center of each tortilla.

- Roll the tortillas tightly around the mixture and place, seam-side down, into the bottom of a 13x9-inch baking dish.
- Sprinkle about 2/3 of the remaining Cheddar cheese over the rolled enchiladas.
- Place the warm chili mixture over the enchiladas evenly, followed by the remaining Cheddar cheese.
- Cook in the oven for about 20-25 minutes.

Amount per serving (5 total)

Timing Information:

Preparation	15 m
Cooking	30 m
Total Time	45 m

Nutritional Information:

Calories	933 kcal
Fat	59 g
Carbohydrates	69.1g
Protein	35.1 g
Cholesterol	108 mg
Sodium	1776 mg

* Percent Daily Values are based on a 2,000 calorie diet.

LONE ★ STATE POTATO SOUP

Ingredients

- 2 potatoes, peeled and cubed
- 1 onion, chopped
- 1 green bell pepper, chopped
- 1 red bell pepper, chopped
- 2 tbsp margarine
- 4 oz. chopped ham
- 1 tbsp chopped green chili peppers
- 1/4 tsp ground white pepper
- 1/8 tsp cayenne pepper
- 1 (14.5 oz.) can chicken broth
- 1 egg yolk, beaten
- 1/4 C. heavy whipping cream
- 1/2 C. shredded Cheddar cheese

Directions

- In a pan of boiling water, cook the potatoes for about 15 minutes.
- Drain and keep aside.
- In a skillet, melt the margarine and sauté the onion and bell peppers for about 10 minutes.

- Stir in the ham, green chilies, white pepper and cayenne and sauté for about 1 minute.
- In a blender, add the potatoes and chicken broth and pulse till smooth.
- Add the potato mixture into the ham mixture and bring to a boil.
- In a small bowl, add the egg yolk and heavy cream and beat to combine.
- Stir in 1/2 C. of the hot soup.
- Stir the yolk mixture into the soup and cook till heated completely.
- Serve with a garnishing of the shredded cheddar cheese.

Amount per serving (6 total)

Timing Information:

Preparation	20 m
Cooking	35 m
Total Time	55 m

Nutritional Information:

Calories	219 kcal
Fat	13.2 g
Carbohydrates	17.7g
Protein	8.2 g
Cholesterol	69 mg
Sodium	379 mg

* Percent Daily Values are based on a 2,000 calorie diet.

Catalina's Stir Fry

Ingredients

- 1 tsp olive oil
- 1 green bell pepper, chopped
- 1 red bell pepper, chopped
- 2 tbsp all-purpose flour
- 1 (1 oz.) packet taco seasoning mix
- 1 lb. skinless, boneless chicken breast halves - cut into bite size pieces
- 2 tsp olive oil
- 1 (15 oz.) can black beans, rinsed and drained
- 1/2 C. prepared salsa
- 1 C. shredded Cheddar cheese

Directions

- In a skillet, heat 1 tsp of the olive oil on medium-high heat and sauté the bell peppers for about 5 minutes.
- Remove from the heat and keep aside.
- In a bowl, mix together the flour and taco seasoning in a bowl.
- Coat the chicken pieces with the flour mixture evenly.
- In a large skillet, heat 2 tsp of the olive oil on medium-high heat and cook the chicken for about 5 minutes.

- Stir in the bell peppers, black beans and salsa and simmer for about 5 minutes.
- Serve with a sprinkling of the Cheddar cheese.

Amount per serving (4 total)

Timing Information:

Preparation	20 m
Cooking	15 m
Total Time	35 m

Nutritional Information:

Calories	333 kcal
Fat	15.9 g
Carbohydrates	13.3g
Protein	32.1 g
Cholesterol	94 mg
Sodium	945 mg

* Percent Daily Values are based on a 2,000 calorie diet.

Quinoa Salad from Mexico

Ingredients

- 1 C. quinoa
- 2 C. water
- 1 tsp kosher salt
- 1/4 C. fresh lime juice
- 2 tbsp olive oil
- 1/8 tsp ground black pepper
- 1 (14 oz.) can diced tomatoes with green chili peppers, drained
- 1 (14 oz.) can garbanzo beans, drained and rinsed
- 1 bunch cilantro, chopped
- 2 avocados, cubed
- 1/4 C. crumbled cotija cheese

Directions

- In a pan, add the quinoa, water and salt and bring to a boil.
- Reduce the heat to medium-low and simmer, covered for about 20-25 minutes.
- Meanwhile in a large bowl, mix together the lime juice, olive oil, pepper, diced tomatoes and garbanzo beans.
- Add the quinoa and stir to combine.

- Refrigerate to cool for about 2 hours.
- With a fork, fluff the quinoa mixture and gently fold in the cilantro, avocados and cheese.

Amount per serving (10 total)

Timing Information:

Preparation	20 m
Cooking	20 m
Total Time	2 h 40 m

Nutritional Information:

Calories	219 kcal
Fat	11.1 g
Carbohydrates	25.7g
Protein	6.3 g
Cholesterol	3 mg
Sodium	515 mg

* Percent Daily Values are based on a 2,000 calorie diet.

Tex Mex Breakfast Eggs

Ingredients

- 1 tbsp butter
- 1 (4 oz.) can chopped green chilis
- 1/2 tomato, chopped
- 6 large eggs
- 1/4 C. crushed tortilla chips
- 1/4 C. shredded sharp Cheddar cheese
- 6 (8 inch) flour tortillas
- 6 tbsp taco sauce

Directions

- In a large skillet, melt the butter on medium heat and cook the green chilis and tomato for about 5 minutes.
- Carefully, crack the eggs into the skillet and stir till the yolks break.
- Cook, stirring for about 2-3 minutes.
- Sprinkle the tortilla chips on top and mix with the eggs.
- Move egg mixture to the side of the skillet and remove from the heat.
- Immediately, sprinkle the Cheddar cheese over the egg mixture and keep aside, covered for about 5 minutes.

- In a microwave-safe plate, place the flour tortillas and microwave for about 30 seconds.
- Divide the egg mixture onto each tortilla and serve with a topping of the taco sauce.

Amount per serving (6 total)

Timing Information:

Preparation	10 m
Cooking	10 m
Total Time	20 m

Nutritional Information:

Calories	283 kcal
Fat	12.2 g
Carbohydrates	30.8g
Protein	12.1 g
Cholesterol	196 mg
Sodium	661 mg

* Percent Daily Values are based on a 2,000 calorie diet.

August's Tex Mex Veggie Casserole

Ingredients

- 1 lb. ground beef
- 1/4 C. olive oil, divided
- 4 zucchini, cut into 1/2-inch cubes
- 1 red bell pepper, chopped
- 1 jalapeno pepper, seeded and chopped
- 4 cloves garlic, minced
- 4 green onions, chopped -- white and green parts separated
- salt and pepper to taste
- 3 tbsp tomato paste
- 4 tsp chili powder
- 2 tsp ground cumin
- 1 (15 oz.) can black beans, rinsed and drained
- 1 (15 oz.) can kidney beans, rinsed and drained
- 1 C. frozen corn, thawed
- 1/2 C. grated Parmesan cheese, divided
- 1/4 C. chopped fresh cilantro

Directions

- Set your oven to 400 degrees F before doing anything else and grease a 13x9-inch baking dish with about 1 tsp of the olive oil.
- Heat a large skillet on medium heat and cook the beef for about 10 minutes.
- Drain the excess grease from the skillet and keep aside.
- Meanwhile in another large skillet, heat the remaining olive oil on medium-high heat and cook the zucchini, red bell pepper, jalapeño pepper, garlic and white parts of the green onions for about 3-5 minutes.
- Stir in the salt, black pepper, tomato paste, chili powder and cumin and simmer for about 1 minute.
- Remove from the heat.
- Add the cooked ground beef, black beans, kidney beans, corn and 1/4 C. of the Parmesan cheese and stir till well combined.
- Transfer the mixture into the prepared baking dish evenly and top with the remaining 1/4 C. of the Parmesan cheese.
- With a foil paper, cover the baking dish and cook in the oven for about 20-25 minutes.
- Remove the foil paper and cook in the oven for about 5-10 minutes.
- Serve with a garnishing of the remaining green onions (green tops) and cilantro.

Amount per serving (8 total)

Timing Information:

Preparation	30 m
Cooking	40 m
Total Time	1 h 10 m

Nutritional Information:

Calories	281 kcal
Fat	15.8 g
Carbohydrates	20g
Protein	17 g
Cholesterol	39 mg
Sodium	298 mg

* Percent Daily Values are based on a 2,000 calorie diet.

TILAPIA SOUTH OF THE BORDER STYLE

Ingredients

- 4 (3 oz.) fresh tilapia fillets
- 1/4 C. olive oil
- 1/4 C. fresh lime juice
- 2 tomatoes, chopped
- 2 fresh jalapeno peppers, sliced into rings
- 8 sprigs cilantro leaves
- salt and ground black pepper to taste

Directions

- In a glass baking dish, arrange the tilapia fillets.
- Drizzle with the olive oil and lime juice evenly and season with the salt and pepper.
- Keep in the room temperature for about 1 hour.
- In a non-stick skillet, place the tilapia fillets on medium heat.
- Pour the lime juice mixture from the baking dish on top.
- Arrange the tomatoes, jalapeños and cilantro over the fillets and cook for about 4 minutes per side.

Amount per serving (4 total)

Timing Information:

Preparation	20 m
Cooking	8 m
Total Time	1 h 28 m

Nutritional Information:

Calories	225 kcal
Fat	14.9 g
Carbohydrates	4.8g
Protein	18.3 g
Cholesterol	31 mg
Sodium	141 mg

* Percent Daily Values are based on a 2,000 calorie diet.

Catalina's Salad

Ingredients

- 1 (15 oz.) can pinto beans, drained and rinsed
- 1 (15 oz.) can black beans, rinsed and drained
- 1 1/2 C. shredded Cheddar and Monterey cheese blend
- 1 (10 oz.) package chopped romaine lettuce
- 3 tomatoes, chopped
- 1 (16 oz.) bottle Catalina salad dressing
- 1 (16 oz.) package corn chips

Directions

- In a large bowl, mix together the pinto beans, black beans, cheese, lettuce and tomatoes.
- Add 3/4 of the bottle of the dressing and mix well.
- Add the corn chips before serving.

Amount per serving (10 total)

Timing Information:

Preparation	
Cooking	5 m
Total Time	5 m

Nutritional Information:

Calories	542 kcal
Fat	33.1 g
Carbohydrates	52.7g
Protein	10.7 g
Cholesterol	12 mg
Sodium	1077 mg

* Percent Daily Values are based on a 2,000 calorie diet.

NACHARITO BAKE

Ingredients

- 1 (10 oz.) bag nacho cheese-flavored corn chips, crushed
- 1 tbsp butter
- 1 small onion, finely chopped
- 1 (14.5 oz.) can diced tomatoes
- 1 (10.75 oz.) can condensed cream of chicken soup
- 1 (10.75 oz.) can cream of mushroom soup
- 1 (4.5 oz.) can chopped green chilis
- 1/3 C. milk
- 2 tbsp sour cream
- 1 tsp chili powder
- 1 tsp ground cumin
- 2 1/2 C. chopped cooked chicken
- 1 (8 oz.) package shredded sharp Cheddar cheese

Directions

- Set your oven to 350 degrees F before doing anything else and lightly, grease a 13x9-inch baking dish.
- Spread the corn chip crumbs in the bottom of the prepared baking dish and press downwards.
- In a large skillet, melt the butter on medium-high heat and sauté the onion for about 6-7 minutes.

- In a large bowl, add the diced tomatoes, cream of chicken soup, cream of mushroom soup, green chilis, milk, sour cream, chili powder, cumin, chicken and cooked onion and stir to combine.
- Place the mixture over the corn chips evenly and top with the Cheddar cheese.
- Cook in the oven for about 55-60 minutes.
- Remove from the oven and keep aside for about 10 minutes before serving.

Amount per serving (8 total)

Timing Information:

Preparation	15 m
Cooking	1 h 5 m
Total Time	1 h 30 m

Nutritional Information:

Calories	480 kcal
Fat	29.5 g
Carbohydrates	31.1g
Protein	24.2 g
Cholesterol	71 mg
Sodium	1209 mg

* Percent Daily Values are based on a 2,000 calorie diet.

La Águila Dip

Ingredients

- 1 lb. ground beef
- 1 tsp chili powder
- 1 (16 oz.) can vegetarian refried beans
- 1 yellow onion, chopped
- 2 (4 oz.) cans chopped green chili peppers, drained
- 1 (16 oz.) jar picante sauce
- 1/2 lb. Muenster cheese, cubed
- 1/2 lb. Monterey Jack cheese, cubed
- 1 (16 oz.) container sour cream
- 5 pieces turkey bacon

Directions

- Set your oven to 350 degrees F before doing anything else.
- Heat a large skillet on medium-high heat and cook the bacon till browned completely.
- Drain the excess grease from the skillet.
- Stir in the chili powder and cook for about 5 minutes.
- In an 8x8-inch baking dish, spread the refried beans, followed by the ground beef mixture, onion, green chili peppers, picante sauce, Muenster cheese and Monterey Jack cheese.

- Cook in the oven for about 35-45 minutes.
- Serve with a topping of the sour cream.

Amount per serving (12 total)

Timing Information:

Preparation	20 m
Cooking	40 m
Total Time	1 h

Nutritional Information:

Calories	390 kcal
Fat	29.8 g
Carbohydrates	11.5g
Protein	19.1 g
Cholesterol	84 mg
Sodium	925 mg

* Percent Daily Values are based on a 2,000 calorie diet.

Chicken Platter

Ingredients

- 3 fresh Poblano chili peppers
- 3 Anaheim chili peppers
- 3/4 lb. tomatillos, diced
- 1 onion, chopped
- 2/3 C. red bell pepper, diced
- 4 green onions, chopped
- 6 cloves garlic, minced
- 1 C. chicken broth
- 3 tbsp vegetable oil
- 4 skinless, boneless chicken breast halves - cut into 2 inch pieces
- 1/4 C. all-purpose flour
- 1 tbsp dried oregano
- 1/2 tsp salt
- 1 pinch black pepper
- 1 pinch cayenne pepper
- 2/3 C. fresh cilantro, chopped

Directions

- Set your oven to 450 degrees F before doing anything else.

- Roast the peppers for about 25 minutes.
- Remove the skin of peppers and then chop them.
- In a pan, add the chopped peppers with tomatillos, onion, red pepper, green onion, garlic and chicken broth and bring to a boil.
- Reduce the heat and simmer for 15 minutes.
- Coat the chicken with the flour evenly.
- In a large skillet, heat the oil on medium heat and sauté the chicken briefly.
- Place the tomatillo mixture over the chicken.
- Stir in the oregano, salt, black pepper and cayenne pepper and simmer for about 25 minutes.
- Stir in the cilantro just before serving.

Amount per serving (4 total)

Timing Information:

Preparation	15 m
Cooking	1 h
Total Time	1 h 15 m

Nutritional Information:

Calories	334 kcal
Fat	13.2 g
Carbohydrates	23.6g
Protein	31.5 g
Cholesterol	68 mg
Sodium	384 mg

* Percent Daily Values are based on a 2,000 calorie diet.

Fruity Guacamole

Ingredients

- 2 ripe Hass avocados - halved, pitted, and peeled
- 2 tomatillos, husked and chopped
- 1 ripe mango - peeled, seeded, and cut into cubes
- 1/2 small red onion, finely chopped
- 1 Serrano chili pepper, finely chopped
- 2 tbsp chopped fresh cilantro
- 1 tbsp chopped fresh mint
- 1 1/2 tbsp fresh lemon juice
- kosher salt to taste

Directions

- In a bowl, add the avocado and salt and with a fork, mash till slightly chunky.
- Add the tomatillos, mango, onion, Serrano chili pepper, cilantro, mint, lemon juice and salt and gently mix.
- Place a plastic wrap over the surface of the guacamole and refrigerate for at least 1 hour.

Amount per serving (8 total)

Timing Information:

Preparation	
Cooking	15 m
Total Time	1 h 15 m

Nutritional Information:

Calories	98 kcal
Fat	7.5 g
Carbohydrates	8.7g
Protein	1.3 g
Cholesterol	0 mg
Sodium	55 mg

* Percent Daily Values are based on a 2,000 calorie diet.

5 Star Salsa

Ingredients

- 6 oz. fresh tomatillos - husked, rinsed, and halved
- 1 tbsp thinly sliced serrano chilis
- 1 large ripe avocado - halved, seeded, and flesh scooped out of peel
- 1/4 C. packed cilantro leaves
- 1/2 lime, juiced
- salt to taste

Directions

- In a food processor, add the tomatillos, Serrano pepper, avocado, cilantro, lime juice and salt and pulse till smooth.
- Transfer the salsa into a serving bowl and serve.

Amount per serving (6 total)

Timing Information:

Preparation	
Cooking	15 m
Total Time	15 m

Nutritional Information:

Calories	87 kcal
Fat	7.3 g
Carbohydrates	6.4g
Protein	1.3 g
Cholesterol	0 mg
Sodium	5 mg

* Percent Daily Values are based on a 2,000 calorie diet.

MUENSTER AND CHILI CHICKEN

Ingredients

- 1.5 C. chicken broth
- 1/2 C. teriyaki sauce
- 1 tbsp chili powder
- 1 tsp garlic powder
- 8 skinless, boneless chicken breast halves
- 8 slices Muenster cheese
- 3 1/2 lb. fresh tomatillos, husks removed
- 1/2 C. water
- 1 onion, chopped
- 6 cloves garlic, chopped
- 1 pinch salt and ground black pepper to taste
- 1/4 C. chopped fresh cilantro
- 1 C. sour cream

Directions

- In a bowl, add the broth, teriyaki sauce, chili powder and garlic powder and beat till well combined.
- Transfer the broth mixture into a resealable plastic bag.
- Add the chicken and coat with the marinade generously.
- Squeeze out the excess air and seal the bag tightly.

- Refrigerator for about 6-24 hours.
- Set your outdoor grill for medium-high heat and lightly, grease the grill grate.
- Remove chicken from the bag and shake off the excess marinade.
- Cook the chicken breasts on grill for about 7-10 minutes per side.
- Arrange the chicken breasts in a baking dish and place a Muenster cheese slice over each breast.
- Set your oven to 350 degrees F.
- In a large pan, add the tomatillos and water and bring to a boil.
- Reduce the heat to medium-low and simmer, covered for about 7-10 minutes.
- Stir in the onion and garlic, salt and pepper and simmer for about 15 minutes.
- In a blender, add the tomatillo sauce mixture and pulse till smooth.
- Stir in the sour cream and cilantro into the tomatillo mixture.
- Place the tomatillo mixture over the chicken and Muenster cheese evenly.
- Cook in the oven for about 15 minutes.

Amount per serving (8 total)

Timing Information:

Preparation	20 m
Cooking	30 m
Total Time	6 h 50 m

Nutritional Information:

Calories	399 kcal
Fat	19.1 g
Carbohydrates	21.8g
Protein	33.4 g
Cholesterol	98 mg
Sodium	948 mg

* Percent Daily Values are based on a 2,000 calorie diet.

Santa Maria Stew

Ingredients

- 2 tbsp lard
- 6 lb. boneless pork shoulder, cubed, optional
- 1 tsp whole coriander seeds
- 2 onions, chopped
- 2 potatoes, cubed
- 2 carrots, chopped
- 5 cloves garlic, chopped
- 1 (18.75 oz.) can tomatillos, coarsely chopped
- 1 (16 oz.) can chopped green chilis
- 1 (11 oz.) can jalapeno peppers, drained and diced
- 1 (30 oz.) jar sliced nopalitos, drained and rinsed
- 2 tsp dried oregano
- 1 (20 oz.) can hominy, drained
- 4 tsp cumin seed
- 2 C. crumbled queso fresco
- 1/2 C. chopped fresh cilantro

Directions

- In a large pan, melt the lard on high heat and cook the cubed pork and coriander seeds for about 10 minutes.

- Stir in the onions, potatoes, carrots, garlic, tomatillos, green chilis, jalapeño peppers, nopalitos, hominy, oregano, cumin seed and water if required and bring to a boil.
- Reduce the heat to medium-low and simmer, covered for about 45 minutes, stirring occasionally.
- Divide the stew into serving bowls and serve with a sprinkle of the crumbled cheese and chopped cilantro.

Amount per serving (12 total)

Timing Information:

Preparation	50 m
Cooking	55 m
Total Time	1 h 45 m

Nutritional Information:

Calories	488 kcal
Fat	28.2 g
Carbohydrates	26.9g
Protein	31.8 g
Cholesterol	105 mg
Sodium	1258 mg

* Percent Daily Values are based on a 2,000 calorie diet.

TOMATILLO STEW

Ingredients

- 20 fresh tomatillos, husks removed
- 2 large tomatoes, chopped
- 7 serrano chili peppers, chopped
- 10 fresh chili de arbol peppers, chopped
- 5 cloves garlic, divided
- salt to taste
- 2 lb. pork stew meat, coarsely chopped, optional

Directions

- In a pan, add the tomatillos, tomatoes, Serrano peppers, chili de arbol peppers and 3 whole garlic cloves on medium-low heat and cook for about 10 minutes.
- Remove the garlic cloves.
- In a blender, add the tomatillo mixture and pulse till smooth.
- Transfer the tomatillo sauce into a bowl.
- Mince 1 garlic clove and mix into the tomatillo sauce with the salt.
- Mince 1 more garlic clove.

- In a skillet, add the pork a minced garlic clove on medium heat and cook, covered for about 30 minutes, stirring occasionally.
- Place the tomatillo sauce over the pork and reduce the heat and simmer for about 5-10 minutes, stirring occasionally.

Amount per serving (4 total)

Timing Information:

Preparation	15 m
Cooking	45 m
Total Time	1 h

Nutritional Information:

Calories	614 kcal
Fat	35.8 g
Carbohydrates	26.1g
Protein	48.6 g
Cholesterol	136 mg
Sodium	108 mg

* Percent Daily Values are based on a 2,000 calorie diet.

Complex Colorado Chili

Ingredients

- 4 fresh tomatillos - husked, peeled, and halved
- 3 Anaheim chili peppers - seeded and halved
- 3 jalapeno peppers - seeded and halved lengthwise
- 1 medium onion, halved
- 1 green bell pepper, seeded and halved lengthwise
- 1 tbsp olive oil
- salt to taste
- 1 tbsp olive oil
- 1 1/2 C. pork shoulder, cut into 1-inch chunks, optional
- salt and ground black pepper to taste
- 2 tomatoes, chopped
- 4 cloves garlic, chopped
- 1 beef bouillon cube
- 1/2 (12 fluid oz.) can lager-style beer
- 2 tbsp chopped fresh oregano
- 1 tbsp chopped fresh parsley
- 1 tbsp ground cumin
- 1 tsp chili powder
- 4 oz. cream cheese at room temperature

Directions

- Set your oven to 425 degrees F before doing anything else.
- In a baking sheet, arrange the halved tomatillos, Anaheim chilis, jalapeño, onion and green bell pepper and drizzle with 1 tbsp of the olive oil.
- Cook in the oven for about 30 minutes.
- Remove from the oven and keep aside to cool.
- After cooling, chop the vegetables into bite-size pieces.
- In a large skillet, heat 1 tbsp of the olive oil on high heat and sear the pork cubes with the salt and black pepper for about 12 minutes.
- Transfer the pork cubes into a slow cooker and roasted vegetables.
- Add the tomatoes, garlic, beef bouillon cube, beer, oregano, parsley, cumin and chili powder and stir to combine.
- Set the slow cooker on Low and cook, covered for about 4-6 hours.
- About 1/2 hour before serving, place the cream cheese into a large bowl.
- Add 1 tbsp of the chili liquid and mix till well combined.
- Slowly, add the chili broth, a tbsp at a time in the cream cheese mixture till it is almost a liquid.
- Add the cream cheese mixture into the chili and stir to combine.

Amount per serving (8 total)

Timing Information:

Preparation	30 m
Cooking	4 h 30 m
Total Time	5 h

Nutritional Information:

Calories	174 kcal
Fat	12 g
Carbohydrates	8.6g
Protein	7.6 g
Cholesterol	32 mg
Sodium	172 mg

* Percent Daily Values are based on a 2,000 calorie diet.

TUESDAY BARCELONA DINNER

Ingredients

- 1/2 lb. dry lentils
- 1 cube chicken bouillon
- 1/2 (1 lb.) Mexican chorizo, casing removed and meat crumbled
- 6 slices turkey bacon
- 1 Roma (plum) tomato, diced
- 1 tomatillo, diced
- 1 small white onion, diced
- 2 cloves garlic, minced
- 1/2 C. water
- 1/2 bunch cilantro, chopped
- 1/8 tsp cumin
- 5 tsp crumbled cotija cheese, divided
- 5 tsp sour cream, divided

Directions

- Rinse the lentils and transfer into a large pan.
- Add the chicken bouillon cube and enough water to cover the lentils by 2-inch and bring to a boil.
- Simmer for about 20 minutes.

- Meanwhile in a large skillet, heat on medium-high heat and cook the chorizo for about 10-15 minutes.
- Transfer the chorizo into a plate.
- In the same pan, cook the bacon for about 5 minutes.
- Transfer the bacon into a plate, leaving the drippings in pan.
- Chop the bacon.
- In the same pan, add the tomato, tomatillo, onion and garlic and cook for about 5 minutes.
- Stir in the water and cilantro and transfer the mixture into a blender and pulses till smooth.
- In the pan of the lentils, add the pureed vegetables, cooked chorizo, cooked bacon and cumin on medium heat and cook for about 5 minutes.
- Divide the lentils mixture in bowls and serve with a topping of the cotija cheese and a dollop of sour cream.

Nutrition

Amount per serving (5 total)

Timing Information:

Preparation	15 m
Cooking	35 m
Total Time	50 m

Nutritional Information:

Calories	528 kcal
Fat	35.1 g
Carbohydrates	27.2g
Protein	26.5 g
Cholesterol	68 mg
Sodium	1078 mg

* Percent Daily Values are based on a 2,000 calorie diet.

November's Tacos

Ingredients

- 1 yam, peeled and diced
- 1 tbsp olive oil
- 3/4 lb. ground turkey
- 1/2 C. chopped sweet onion
- 1 clove garlic, minced
- 4 jalapeno peppers, seeded and minced
- 1 tbsp chili powder
- 1 tsp ground cumin
- 1/2 tsp Cajun seasoning
- 1/2 tsp salt
- 1/2 C. tomatillo salsa
- 1/2 C. chopped fresh cilantro
- 16 warm flour tortillas

Directions

- In a microwave safe bowl, add the diced yam and microwave for about 5-7 minutes, stirring once in the middle way.
- In a large skillet, heat the olive oil on medium heat and cook the turkey for about 5-7 minutes.

- Add the onion, garlic, and jalapeño pepper and cook for about 7-10 minutes.
- Stir in the chili powder, cumin, Cajun seasoning and salt and top with the salsa.
- Fold in the yam and cook till the excess moisture is absorbed.
- Top with the cilantro and serve with the warm tortillas.

Amount per serving (8 total)

Timing Information:

Preparation	20 m
Cooking	25 m
Total Time	45 m

Nutritional Information:

Calories	602 kcal
Fat	16.4 g
Carbohydrates	91.1g
Protein	21.6 g
Cholesterol	31 mg
Sodium	1182 mg

* Percent Daily Values are based on a 2,000 calorie diet.

Restaurant-Style Salsa

Ingredients

- 10 fresh tomatillos, husks removed
- 3 cloves garlic
- 1 C. water
- 4 serrano chilis, stemmed
- 2 Poblano chilis, stemmed
- 3 tbsp vegetable oil
- 1 yellow onion, chopped
- 1 tsp coarse salt
- 1/4 C. chopped fresh cilantro
- 2 tbsp minced red onion
- 1 tbsp fresh lime juice

Directions

- In a pan, add the tomatillos, garlic cloves and water on high heat and bring to a boil.
- Reduce the heat to medium-low and simmer for about 15-20 minutes.
- Set the broiler of your oven and arrange oven rack about 6-inches from the heating element.
- Line a baking sheet with a piece of foil.

- Cut the Serrano peppers and Poblano peppers in half from top to bottom.
- Remove the stem, seeds and ribs.
- Arrange the peppers, cut-side-down onto the prepared baking sheet.
- Cook under the broiler for about 3-5 minutes.
- Remove from the oven and transfer into a bowl.
- Immediately with a plastic wrap, seal the bowl tightly and keep aside for about 5-7 minutes.
- Remove the blackened skins from the peppers.
- Add the peppers into the simmering tomatillos mixture and cook for about 5 minutes.
- In a skillet, heat the vegetable oil on medium heat and sauté the yellow onion for about 7-10 minutes.
- In a blender, add the yellow onions and tomatillo mixture and pulse till smooth.
- Return the mixture into the skillet on medium-high heat and simmer for about 5-7 minutes.
- Transfer the mixture into a bowl and keep aside to cool in room temperature.
- After cooling, stir in the salt, cilantro, red onion and lime juice and serve.

Amount per serving (15 total)

Timing Information:

Preparation	20 m
Cooking	30 m
Total Time	2 h

Nutritional Information:

Calories	40 kcal
Fat	3 g
Carbohydrates	3.2g
Protein	0.6 g
Cholesterol	0 mg
Sodium	120 mg

* Percent Daily Values are based on a 2,000 calorie diet.

HOMEMADE FAJITA SPICE MIX

Ingredients

- 1 tbsp cornstarch
- 2 tsp chili powder
- 1 tsp salt
- 1 tsp paprika
- 1 tsp white sugar
- 1/2 tsp onion powder
- 1/2 tsp garlic powder
- 1/4 tsp cayenne pepper
- 1/2 tsp ground cumin

Directions

- In a small bowl, add all the ingredients and mix well.

Amount per serving (4 total)

Timing Information:

Preparation	
Cooking	5 m
Total Time	5 m

Nutritional Information:

Calories	21 kcal
Fat	0.4 g
Carbohydrates	4.6g
Protein	0.4 g
Cholesterol	0 mg
Sodium	596 mg

* Percent Daily Values are based on a 2,000 calorie diet.

Snow Belt Fajitas

Ingredients

Fajita Seasoning:

- 2 tsp seasoned salt
- 1/4 tsp garlic salt
- 1/2 tsp black pepper
- 1/2 tsp cayenne pepper
- 1 tsp dried oregano
- 1 1/2 lb. venison, cut into 2 inch strips
- 4 tbsp vegetable oil
- 1 medium red bell pepper, cut into 2 inch strips
- 1 medium yellow bell pepper, cut into 2 inch strips
- 1 medium onion, cut into 1/2-inch wedges
- 12 fajita size flour tortillas, warmed

Directions

- For the fajita seasoning in a bowl, mix together the seasoned salt, garlic salt, black pepper, cayenne pepper and oregano.
- Sprinkle 2 tsp of the seasoning over the sliced venison and mix well.
- Refrigerate, covered for about 30 minutes.

- In a heavy frying pan, heat 2 tbsp of the oil and sauté the bell pepper and onion till tender.
- Transfer the bell pepper mixture into a bowl.
- In the same skillet, heat the remaining oil and cook the venison till browned.
- Add the bell pepper mixture and remaining fajita seasoning and cook till heated through.
- Served with the warmed tortillas.

Amount per serving (6 total)

Timing Information:

Preparation	30 m
Cooking	15 m
Total Time	45 m

Nutritional Information:

Calories	688 kcal
Fat	23.2 g
Carbohydrates	78.8g
Protein	38.7 g
Cholesterol	96 mg
Sodium	1357 mg

* Percent Daily Values are based on a 2,000 calorie diet.

Zucchini Black Bean Veggie Fajitas

Ingredients

- 1/4 C. olive oil
- 1/4 C. red wine vinegar
- 1 tsp dried oregano
- 1 tsp chili powder
- garlic salt to taste
- salt and pepper to taste
- 1 tsp white sugar
- 2 small zucchini, julienned
- 2 medium small yellow squash, julienned
- 1 large onion, sliced
- 1 green bell pepper, cut into thin strips
- 1 red bell pepper, cut into thin strips
- 2 tbsp olive oil
- 1 (8.75 oz.) can whole kernel corn, drained
- 1 (15 oz.) can black beans, drained

Directions

- In a large bowl mix together the olive oil, vinegar, oregano, chili powder, garlic salt, salt, pepper and sugar.

- Add the zucchini, yellow squash, onion, green pepper and red pepper and coat with the oil mixture.
- Refrigerate to marinate for at least 30 minutes.
- Remove the vegetables from the refrigerator and drain well.
- In a large skillet, heat the oil on medium-high heat and sauté the vegetables for about 10-15 minutes.
- Stir in the corn and beans and increase the heat to high.
- Cook for about 5 minutes.

Amount per serving (6 total)

Timing Information:

Preparation	20 m
Cooking	20 m
Total Time	1 h 10 m

Nutritional Information:

Calories	198 kcal
Fat	14.4 g
Carbohydrates	17.9g
Protein	3 g
Cholesterol	0 mg
Sodium	130 mg

* Percent Daily Values are based on a 2,000 calorie diet.

New York Fajitas

Ingredients

- 1/4 C. olive oil
- 1 lime, juiced
- 3 tbsp chopped fresh cilantro
- 2 tbsp finely chopped onion
- 3 cloves garlic, finely chopped
- 1 1/2 tsp ground cumin
- 1 tsp salt
- 1 tsp ground black pepper
- 2 (8 oz.) boneless New York strip steaks, cut into thin strips
- 8 (6 inch) white corn tortillas
- 1 (8 oz.) jar salsa
- 1 (8 oz.) package shredded Mexican cheese blend

Directions

- In a bowl, add the olive oil, lime juice, cilantro, onion, garlic, cumin, salt and black pepper and beat till well combined.
- Transfer the mixture into a resealable plastic bag.
- Add the steak strips and coat with the marinade generously.

- Squeeze out the excess air and seal the bag.
- Refrigerate to marinate for about 4 hours to overnight.
- Heat a large skillet over medium heat and cook the beef for 15-20 minutes.
- Serve the cooked beef with the tortillas, salsa and Mexican cheese blend.

Amount per serving (4 total)

Timing Information:

Preparation	15 m
Cooking	15 m
Total Time	4 h 30 m

Nutritional Information:

Calories	699 kcal
Fat	42.3 g
Carbohydrates	31.3g
Protein	49.8 g
Cholesterol	121 mg
Sodium	1451 mg

* Percent Daily Values are based on a 2,000 calorie diet.

MEXICAN BEEF MARINADE

Ingredients

- 1/4 C. lime juice
- 1/4 C. olive oil
- 1/3 C. water
- 1 tbsp vinegar
- 2 tsp soy sauce
- 2 tsp Worcestershire sauce
- 1 clove garlic, minced
- 1/2 tsp chili powder
- 1/2 tsp beef bouillon paste
- 1/2 tsp ground cumin
- 1/2 tsp dried oregano
- 1/4 tsp ground black pepper
- 1 pinch onion powder

Directions

- In a bowl, add all the ingredients and beat till well combined.

Amount per serving (4 total)

Timing Information:

Preparation	
Cooking	10 m
Total Time	10 m

Nutritional Information:

Calories	132 kcal
Fat	13.7 g
Carbohydrates	3g
Protein	0.4 g
Cholesterol	0 mg
Sodium	182 mg

* Percent Daily Values are based on a 2,000 calorie diet.

QUESADILLAS X FAJITAS

Ingredients

- 2 tbsp vegetable oil, divided
- 1/2 onion, sliced
- 1/2 green bell pepper, sliced
- salt to taste
- 4 flour tortillas
- 1/2 lb. cooked steak, cut into 1/4-inch thick pieces
- 1 C. shredded Mexican cheese blend

Directions

- In a 10-inch skillet, heat 2 tsp of the oil on medium heat and sauté the onion and green bell pepper for about 5-10 minutes.
- Stir in the salt and transfer the mixture into a bowl.
- Brush 1 side of each tortilla with the remaining oil.
- In the same skillet, place 1 tortilla, oil-side down on medium heat.
- Sprinkle with 1/2 of the steak, 1/2 of the onion mixture and 1/2 of the Mexican cheese mixture.
- Place a second tortilla, oil-side up onto the cheese layer, pressing down with a spatula to seal.
- Cook the quesadilla for about 3-4 minutes per side.

- Remove the quesadilla from skillet and cut into wedges.
- Repeat with the remaining ingredients for second quesadilla.

Amount per serving (4 total)

Timing Information:

Preparation	10 m
Cooking	15 m
Total Time	25 m

Nutritional Information:

Calories	552 kcal
Fat	31.1 g
Carbohydrates	40g
Protein	28 g
Cholesterol	79 mg
Sodium	859 mg

* Percent Daily Values are based on a 2,000 calorie diet.

EAST LA FAJITAS

Ingredients

Marinade:

- 4 cloves garlic
- 1 tbsp kosher salt
- 3 tbsp lime juice
- 3 tbsp olive oil
- 3 tbsp minced fresh cilantro
- 1 tsp chili powder
- 1/2 tsp white sugar
- 1/2 tsp paprika
- 1/4 tsp cayenne pepper
- 1 1/2 lb. beef skirt steak, cut across the grain into 1/4-inch strips
- 6 whole wheat tortillas
- 1 tbsp canola oil, divided
- 1 large onion, cut into slices
- 1 red bell pepper, cut into strips
- 1 clove garlic, minced
- 1/4 tsp salt

Directions

- With a mortar and pestle, grind the garlic with the salt till a paste forms.
- In a bowl, add the garlic paste, lime juice, olive oil, cilantro, chili powder, sugar, paprika and cayenne pepper and beat well.
- Transfer the marinade into a resealable plastic bag.
- Add the skirt steak strips and coat with the marinade.
- Squeeze out the excess air and seal the bag.
- Refrigerate to marinate for about 2 hours to overnight.
- Remove the steak from marinade and shake off the excess.
- Set your oven to 300 degrees F.
- Wrap the tortillas tightly in aluminum foil to form a packet and arrange the packet on a baking sheet.
- Cook in the oven for about 10 minutes.
- Remove from the oven and keep warm.
- In a large skillet, heat 1 tsp of the canola oil on high heat and sauté the onion and bell pepper for about 4-5 minutes.
- Transfer the onion mixture into a plate.
- In the same skillet, heat 1 tsp of the canola oil on high heat and cook 1/2 of the steak for about 4-6 minutes.
- Transfer the steak into the plate with the onion mixture.
- In the same skillet, heat the remaining canola oil and cook the remaining steak for about 4-6 minutes.

- Stir in the minced garlic, salt, cooked steak, onion mixture and any accumulated juices and cook till fragrant and heated completely.
- Remove from the heat and divide the steak mixture between the warm tortillas.

Amount per serving (4 total)

Timing Information:

Preparation	15 m
Cooking	25 m
Total Time	2 h 40 m

Nutritional Information:

Calories	453 kcal
Fat	21.8 g
Carbohydrates	48.1g
Protein	27.4 g
Cholesterol	38 mg
Sodium	1974 mg

* Percent Daily Values are based on a 2,000 calorie diet.

THANKS FOR READING! JOIN THE CLUB AND KEEP ON COOKING WITH 6 MORE COOKBOOKS....

http://bit.ly/1TdrStv

 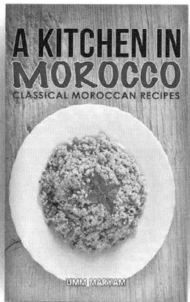 

To grab the box sets simply follow the link mentioned above, or tap one of book covers.

This will take you to a page where you can simply enter your email address and a PDF version of the box sets will be emailed to you.

Hope you are ready for some serious cooking!

http://bit.ly/1TdrStv

Come On...
Let's Be Friends :)

We adore our readers and love connecting with them socially.

Like BookSumo on Facebook and let's get social!

Facebook

And also check out the BookSumo Cooking Blog.

Food Lover Blog